EMMANUEL JOSEPH

Climate Chic, Adaptive Fashion in a Digital Era

Copyright © 2025 by Emmanuel Joseph

All rights reserved. No part of this publication may be reproduced, stored or transmitted in any form or by any means, electronic, mechanical, photocopying, recording, scanning, or otherwise without written permission from the publisher. It is illegal to copy this book, post it to a website, or distribute it by any other means without permission.

First edition

This book was professionally typeset on Reedsy.
Find out more at reedsy.com

Contents

1	Chapter 1: Fashion Forward: The Intersection of Climate and...	1
2	Chapter 2: The Rise of Eco-Friendly Materials	3
3	Chapter 3: Fashion Tech: Innovations Shaping the Future	5
4	Chapter 4: The Power of Circular Fashion	7
5	Chapter 5: Digital Fashion Shows: A Sustainable Revolution	9
6	Chapter 6: The Role of Consumer Behavior in Fashion...	11
7	Chapter 7: Ethical Production: The Heart of Sustainable...	13
8	Chapter 8: Slow Fashion: Embracing Quality Over Quantity	15
9	Chapter 9: The Impact of Fashion on Climate Change	17
10	Chapter 10: The Future of Adaptive Fashion	19
11	Chapter 11: Sustainable Fashion Entrepreneurship: Building a...	21
12	Chapter 12: The Role of Education in Promoting Sustainable...	23
13	Chapter 13: Collaborative Efforts for a Sustainable Future	25
14	Chapter 14: The Role of Policy and Regulation in Sustainable...	27
15	Chapter 15: The Journey Ahead: Embracing Climate Chic	29

1

Chapter 1: Fashion Forward: The Intersection of Climate and Style

Fashion has long been a reflection of society's values and challenges. As climate change becomes a pressing global issue, the fashion industry has a significant role to play in advocating for sustainability. In the digital era, fashion brands are leveraging technology to create climate-conscious collections that are not only stylish but also environmentally friendly. The shift from fast fashion to sustainable fashion marks a pivotal moment where consumers are increasingly aware of the impact their choices have on the planet. The rise of eco-friendly materials and innovative designs has paved the way for a new era of adaptive fashion that champions both style and sustainability.

One remarkable story is that of Stella McCartney, a designer renowned for her commitment to ethical fashion. McCartney's journey began in the early 2000s when she launched her eponymous brand, vowing never to use leather or fur. Her groundbreaking approach to sustainable fashion garnered immense attention, leading her to collaborate with global brands like Adidas to create eco-friendly collections. McCartney's journey exemplifies the power of fashion to drive positive change and inspire others to adopt more sustainable practices. Her brand has become a beacon of hope in the industry, showcasing that fashion and sustainability can go hand in hand without compromising on style.

The digital era has further revolutionized the fashion landscape, enabling brands to connect with consumers on a deeper level. Social media platforms have become powerful tools for raising awareness about climate change and promoting sustainable fashion choices. Influencers and activists use their online presence to advocate for eco-friendly lifestyles, encouraging their followers to make conscious decisions when it comes to their wardrobes. The ability to instantly share information and engage with a global audience has empowered fashion brands to spread their message of sustainability far and wide.

In addition to social media, technology has also played a crucial role in the development of sustainable fashion. Innovations such as 3D printing and virtual reality have opened up new possibilities for designers to create and showcase their collections in ways that were previously unimaginable. These advancements have not only reduced waste but also allowed for more personalized and adaptable fashion experiences. As the fashion industry continues to embrace these technologies, the potential for creating climate-conscious designs becomes limitless.

As we move forward, it is essential to recognize the importance of adaptive fashion in addressing climate change. By embracing sustainable practices and leveraging technology, the fashion industry can lead the way in promoting a more environmentally friendly future. The journey towards climate chic is just beginning, and it is up to both designers and consumers to ensure that fashion remains a force for good in the fight against climate change.

2

Chapter 2: The Rise of Eco-Friendly Materials

The shift towards sustainability in the fashion industry has led to the development and adoption of eco-friendly materials. From organic cotton to recycled polyester, designers are constantly exploring new ways to create stylish garments that have minimal impact on the environment. The quest for sustainable materials has given rise to innovative textiles that are not only kinder to the planet but also enhance the overall quality and durability of fashion products.

One notable material that has gained popularity in recent years is Tencel, a fiber made from sustainably sourced wood pulp. Tencel is known for its softness, breathability, and biodegradability, making it an ideal choice for eco-conscious designers. The story of Tencel's development is one of innovation and perseverance. In the early 1990s, Austrian company Lenzing embarked on a mission to create a sustainable alternative to traditional fibers. After years of research and development, they successfully introduced Tencel to the market, revolutionizing the fashion industry with a material that combines comfort, performance, and sustainability.

Another exciting development in the world of eco-friendly materials is the use of mushroom leather. This innovative material is made from mycelium, the root structure of mushrooms, and offers a sustainable alternative to animal leather. The production process of mushroom leather is significantly less resource-intensive compared to traditional leather, making it an attractive option for environmentally conscious designers. One inspiring story is that of MycoWorks, a company that has been at the forefront of developing and commercializing mushroom leather. Their dedication to creating high-quality, sustainable materials has garnered attention from major fashion brands, paving the way for the widespread adoption of this revolutionary material.

In addition to plant-based materials, the fashion industry is also exploring the potential of recycled fibers. Recycled polyester, for example, is made from post-consumer plastic bottles, offering a sustainable solution to the problem of plastic waste. The journey of transforming plastic waste into wearable garments is a testament to the power of innovation in driving sustainability. Companies like Patagonia have been pioneers in this field, using recycled polyester in their products since the early 1990s. Their commitment to environmental stewardship has set a high standard for the industry, inspiring other brands to follow suit.

The digital era has further facilitated the development and adoption of eco-friendly materials. Advanced technologies such as artificial intelligence and blockchain are being used to trace the origins of materials and ensure transparency in the supply chain. These technologies enable consumers to make informed decisions about the products they purchase, promoting a more sustainable and ethical fashion industry. As the demand for eco-friendly materials continues to grow, it is essential for designers, manufacturers, and consumers to work together in creating a more sustainable future.

The rise of eco-friendly materials marks a significant step forward in the journey towards climate chic. By embracing innovation and prioritizing sustainability, the fashion industry can create stylish garments that not only look good but also do good for the planet. The future of fashion lies in our ability to adapt and evolve, ensuring that style and sustainability go hand in hand.

3

Chapter 3: Fashion Tech: Innovations Shaping the Future

The convergence of fashion and technology is propelling the industry into a new era of innovation and sustainability. From smart textiles to wearable tech, the possibilities are endless, and the potential for positive environmental impact is significant. These advancements are redefining how we interact with fashion, making it more adaptable, personalized, and eco-friendly.

One exciting innovation is the development of smart textiles that can adjust to changing weather conditions. Companies like Google and Levi's have collaborated to create clothing that integrates technology with everyday wear. Their Project Jacquard resulted in a denim jacket that can control your smartphone, offering a glimpse into the future of fashion where technology and clothing are seamlessly integrated. This not only adds convenience but also reduces the need for multiple garments, promoting a more sustainable approach to fashion consumption.

Another groundbreaking development is the use of 3D printing in fashion design. This technology allows designers to create intricate patterns and structures that would be impossible with traditional methods. It also significantly reduces waste, as garments can be produced on-demand, eliminating excess inventory. A notable example is the work of designer Iris van Herpen, who has been a pioneer in incorporating 3D printing into her haute couture collections. Her innovative designs challenge conventional fashion norms and showcase the endless possibilities of combining technology with creativity.

Virtual reality (VR) and augmented reality (AR) are also transforming the fashion industry by offering new ways to experience and shop for clothes. Virtual fitting rooms allow customers to try on clothes without leaving their homes, reducing the need for physical samples and returns. Brands like Gucci and Tommy Hilfiger have embraced AR technology, enabling customers to visualize how garments will look and fit in real-time. This not only enhances the shopping experience but also supports sustainable practices by minimizing the environmental impact of manufacturing and shipping.

The digital era has also given rise to blockchain technology, which is being used to ensure transparency and traceability in the fashion supply chain. Blockchain allows consumers to track the journey of a garment from raw materials to finished product, providing assurance that it was produced ethically and sustainably. This level of transparency empowers consumers to make informed choices and holds brands accountable for their environmental and social impact. The fashion industry is increasingly adopting blockchain to promote trust and integrity, fostering a more sustainable and ethical marketplace.

As fashion tech continues to evolve, it is essential for designers and consumers to embrace these innovations and harness their potential for positive change. By integrating technology with sustainable practices, the fashion industry can lead the way in creating a more environmentally friendly and socially responsible future. The journey towards climate chic is not just about adapting to the changing climate but also about leveraging technology to redefine fashion for the better.

4

Chapter 4: The Power of Circular Fashion

Circular fashion is an emerging concept that aims to create a closed-loop system where garments are designed, produced, and recycled in a way that minimizes waste and environmental impact. This approach challenges the traditional linear fashion model, which often results in massive amounts of waste and pollution. By adopting circular fashion principles, the industry can significantly reduce its ecological footprint and promote a more sustainable future.

A key aspect of circular fashion is the use of recyclable and biodegradable materials. Designers are increasingly turning to materials that can be easily broken down and repurposed at the end of their lifecycle. One inspiring story is that of the brand Reformation, which has been at the forefront of the circular fashion movement. Reformation's commitment to sustainability is evident in their use of eco-friendly materials and their efforts to create a closed-loop system for their garments. Their innovative approach has garnered a loyal following and set a high standard for the industry.

Another important element of circular fashion is the promotion of repair and reuse. Instead of discarding garments after a few wears, consumers are encouraged to repair and repurpose them. This not only extends the lifespan of the clothing but also reduces the demand for new products. Brands like Patagonia have long championed the idea of repair and reuse, offering repair services and encouraging customers to buy used items through their Worn

Wear program. Their dedication to circular fashion has not only strengthened their brand identity but also inspired others to adopt similar practices.

The digital era has also facilitated the growth of circular fashion through the rise of online resale platforms. Websites and apps like Depop, Poshmark, and ThredUp have made it easier than ever for consumers to buy and sell second-hand clothing. These platforms promote a more sustainable approach to fashion consumption by giving garments a second life and reducing the need for new production. The success of these platforms highlights the growing demand for sustainable fashion options and the potential for circular fashion to become mainstream.

As circular fashion continues to gain momentum, it is essential for both designers and consumers to embrace this approach and work towards creating a more sustainable industry. By prioritizing repair, reuse, and recycling, the fashion industry can significantly reduce its environmental impact and pave the way for a more sustainable future. The journey towards climate chic is not just about creating new garments but also about rethinking how we use and value the clothes we already have.

5

Chapter 5: Digital Fashion Shows: A Sustainable Revolution

The traditional fashion show has long been a cornerstone of the industry, showcasing the latest collections from designers and setting the trends for the upcoming season. However, the environmental impact of these events is significant, with travel, production, and waste all contributing to the industry's carbon footprint. In response, many fashion brands are turning to digital fashion shows as a more sustainable alternative.

Digital fashion shows offer a unique opportunity to showcase collections in a way that is both innovative and eco-friendly. By leveraging technology, designers can create immersive virtual experiences that reach a global audience without the need for physical events. One notable example is the 2020 Met Gala, which transitioned to a digital format due to the COVID-19 pandemic. The virtual event featured a series of online exhibitions and performances, highlighting the potential for digital fashion shows to engage and inspire audiences in new ways.

The rise of digital fashion shows has also led to the development of virtual garments, which can be worn and displayed in digital spaces. This innovative approach not only reduces the need for physical production but also offers a new level of creativity and expression. Designers like The Fabricant have been pioneers in creating virtual couture, pushing the boundaries of fashion and technology. Their digital garments are not only visually stunning but also highlight the potential for virtual fashion to reduce the industry's environmental impact.

In addition to reducing waste and emissions, digital fashion shows also offer greater accessibility and inclusivity. Traditional fashion shows are often exclusive events, with limited access for the general public. Digital shows, on the other hand, can be accessed by anyone with an internet connection, democratizing the fashion experience and allowing a wider audience to engage with the latest trends. This increased accessibility promotes diversity and inclusion, ensuring that fashion is a space for everyone.

The digital era has also enabled brands to experiment with new formats and storytelling techniques. From interactive videos to virtual reality experiences, the possibilities for digital fashion shows are endless. Brands like Balenciaga have embraced this new medium, creating immersive virtual experiences that captivate and engage their audience. These innovative approaches not only showcase the latest collections but also offer a glimpse into the future of fashion, where technology and creativity go hand in hand.

As digital fashion shows continue to evolve, it is essential for the industry to embrace this sustainable and innovative approach. By leveraging technology to create engaging and eco-friendly experiences, the fashion industry can reduce its environmental impact and promote a more sustainable future. The journey towards climate chic is not just about adapting to the changing climate but also about rethinking how we showcase and consume fashion in the digital era.

6

Chapter 6: The Role of Consumer Behavior in Fashion Sustainability

The fashion industry is driven by consumer demand, and the choices we make as consumers have a significant impact on the environment. As awareness of climate change and sustainability grows, more people are seeking out eco-friendly fashion options and making conscious decisions about their wardrobes. Understanding the role of consumer behavior in fashion sustainability is essential for driving positive change and promoting a more environmentally friendly industry.

One important aspect of sustainable consumer behavior is the shift towards minimalism and capsule wardrobes. Instead of constantly buying new clothes, consumers are embracing the idea of owning fewer, high-quality pieces that can be mixed and matched to create a variety of outfits. This approach not only reduces waste but also encourages a more thoughtful and intentional approach to fashion consumption. Brands like Everlane have capitalized on this trend by offering timeless, versatile pieces that prioritize quality and sustainability.

The digital era has also empowered consumers to make more informed choices about the products they buy. Online platforms and apps provide a wealth of information about the environmental and social impact of fashion brands, enabling consumers to support companies that align with their values.

Apps like Good On You offer ratings and reviews of fashion brands based on their sustainability practices, helping consumers make more conscious decisions. This increased transparency and access to information are driving demand for sustainable fashion and encouraging brands to adopt more eco-friendly practices.

Another important factor in sustainable consumer behavior is the rise of second-hand and vintage fashion. Thrifting has become a popular trend, with consumers seeking out unique, pre-loved pieces that reduce the need for new production. The success of online resale platforms like Depop and Poshmark highlights the growing demand for second-hand fashion and the potential for circular fashion to become mainstream. By choosing to buy second-hand, consumers can significantly reduce their environmental impact and support a more sustainable industry.

As consumers become more aware of the environmental impact of their fashion choices, they are also demanding greater transparency and accountability from brands. Ethical consumerism is on the rise, with people seeking out companies that prioritize sustainability, fair labor practices, and social responsibility. This shift in consumer behavior is driving brands to adopt more sustainable practices and align their values with those of their customers. The power of consumer demand cannot be underestimated, and it is essential for the fashion industry to listen and respond to the growing call for sustainability.

Understanding the role of consumer behavior in fashion sustainability is crucial for driving positive change and promoting a more environmentally friendly industry. By making conscious choices and supporting brands that prioritize sustainability.

7

Chapter 7: Ethical Production: The Heart of Sustainable Fashion

Sustainable fashion is not just about the materials used in garments; it's also about how those garments are produced. Ethical production practices are at the heart of creating a sustainable fashion industry, ensuring that the people who make our clothes are treated fairly and that the environmental impact of production is minimized. This chapter explores the importance of ethical production and highlights some inspiring stories of brands that are leading the way in this area.

One notable example is the brand People Tree, which has been a pioneer in ethical fashion for over two decades. Founded by Safia Minney in 1991, People Tree has built its business on the principles of fair trade, transparency, and environmental sustainability. The brand works closely with artisans and farmers in developing countries, ensuring that they receive fair wages and work in safe conditions. People Tree's commitment to ethical production has not only set a high standard for the industry but also demonstrated that fashion can be a force for good.

The digital era has also facilitated greater transparency in the fashion supply chain, enabling consumers to make more informed choices about the products they buy. Brands like Everlane have embraced this trend, providing detailed information about the cost and production process of each item they sell. By sharing the stories of the people who make their clothes and the factories where they are produced, Everlane has built a loyal customer base that values transparency and ethical production. This approach not only promotes trust and accountability but also encourages other brands to adopt similar practices.

Another important aspect of ethical production is the use of sustainable manufacturing processes. Brands like Eileen Fisher have made significant strides in reducing the environmental impact of their production methods. Eileen Fisher's Renew program, for example, takes back worn garments from customers and either refurbishes them for resale or recycles the materials to create new products. This closed-loop system not only reduces waste but also ensures that the resources used in production are maximized.

The rise of digital tools and technologies has further enabled brands to adopt more sustainable production practices. From using renewable energy in factories to implementing water-saving techniques, technology is playing a crucial role in reducing the environmental footprint of fashion production. Brands like Patagonia have been at the forefront of this movement, continuously exploring new ways to minimize their impact on the planet. Their commitment to environmental stewardship has not only strengthened their brand identity but also inspired others to follow suit.

As consumers become more aware of the importance of ethical production, it is essential for the fashion industry to continue prioritizing these practices. By supporting brands that prioritize fair labor practices and sustainable production methods, consumers can drive positive change and promote a more ethical and environmentally friendly industry. The journey towards climate chic is not just about creating stylish garments but also about ensuring that those garments are produced in a way that respects both people and the planet.

8

Chapter 8: Slow Fashion: Embracing Quality Over Quantity

The slow fashion movement advocates for a more thoughtful and deliberate approach to fashion consumption, emphasizing quality over quantity. In contrast to fast fashion, which encourages the rapid production and disposal of cheap garments, slow fashion promotes the idea of investing in well-made, timeless pieces that can be worn and cherished for years. This chapter explores the principles of slow fashion and the benefits it offers for both consumers and the environment.

One inspiring story is that of the brand Loro Piana, which has built its reputation on producing high-quality, luxurious garments that stand the test of time. Founded in Italy in 1924, Loro Piana has remained committed to using the finest materials and craftsmanship in their products. Their dedication to quality has earned them a loyal customer base and set a high standard for the industry. By focusing on timeless design and exceptional craftsmanship, Loro Piana exemplifies the principles of slow fashion.

The digital era has also facilitated the growth of the slow fashion movement, enabling consumers to connect with brands that prioritize quality and sustainability. Online platforms like The RealReal and Vestiaire Collective offer a curated selection of pre-owned luxury items, providing consumers with access to high-quality, timeless pieces at a fraction of the original cost.

These platforms not only promote the idea of investing in quality but also support the circular fashion movement by giving garments a second life.

Another important aspect of slow fashion is the emphasis on mindful consumption. Instead of constantly buying new clothes, slow fashion encourages consumers to take a more thoughtful approach to their wardrobes, considering the impact of their choices on the environment and the people who make their clothes. This shift in mindset can lead to a more sustainable and fulfilling relationship with fashion, where each purchase is made with intention and care.

The rise of digital tools and technologies has further enabled consumers to make more informed choices about the products they buy. From online reviews to transparency apps, there are now numerous resources available to help consumers identify brands that align with their values. By supporting companies that prioritize quality and sustainability, consumers can drive positive change and promote a more ethical and environmentally friendly fashion industry.

As the slow fashion movement continues to gain momentum, it is essential for both designers and consumers to embrace this approach and work towards creating a more sustainable industry. By prioritizing quality over quantity and making mindful choices, we can reduce the environmental impact of our fashion consumption and promote a more sustainable future. The journey towards climate chic is not just about keeping up with the latest trends but also about making choices that reflect our values and respect the planet.

9

Chapter 9: The Impact of Fashion on Climate Change

The fashion industry has a significant impact on climate change, with its production processes and consumption patterns contributing to greenhouse gas emissions, water pollution, and resource depletion. Understanding the environmental impact of fashion is essential for driving positive change and promoting a more sustainable industry. This chapter explores the various ways in which fashion affects the climate and highlights some inspiring stories of brands that are working to reduce their environmental footprint.

One notable example is the brand Stella McCartney, which has been a leader in sustainable fashion for over two decades. McCartney's commitment to environmental sustainability is evident in every aspect of her brand, from the materials used in her collections to the production processes employed in her factories. By prioritizing eco-friendly practices and continuously seeking out innovative solutions, Stella McCartney has set a high standard for the industry and demonstrated that fashion can be both stylish and sustainable.

The digital era has also facilitated greater awareness of the environmental impact of fashion, enabling consumers to make more informed choices about the products they buy. Social media platforms, online documentaries, and transparency apps have all played a role in educating the public about the true cost of fashion. Brands like Patagonia have embraced this trend, using their online presence to raise awareness about environmental issues and promote sustainable practices. Their dedication to environmental stewardship has not only strengthened their brand identity but also inspired others to adopt similar practices.

Another important aspect of reducing the environmental impact of fashion is the adoption of sustainable manufacturing processes. From using renewable energy in factories to implementing water-saving techniques, technology is playing a crucial role in minimizing the industry's ecological footprint. Brands like Eileen Fisher have been at the forefront of this movement, continuously exploring new ways to reduce their impact on the planet. Their commitment to sustainability has not only earned them a loyal customer base but also set a high standard for the industry.

The rise of circular fashion has also played a significant role in reducing the environmental impact of fashion. By promoting repair, reuse, and recycling, circular fashion aims to create a closed-loop system where garments are designed, produced, and repurposed in a way that minimizes waste and resource consumption. Brands like Reformation and Patagonia have been pioneers in this field, demonstrating the potential for circular fashion to become mainstream. Their innovative approaches have not only reduced waste but also inspired other brands to adopt similar practices.

As consumers become more aware of the environmental impact of their fashion choices, it is essential for the industry to continue prioritizing sustainability. By supporting brands that prioritize eco-friendly practices and making conscious choices about the products we buy, we can drive positive change and promote a more sustainable future. The journey towards climate chic is not just about creating stylish garments but also about ensuring that those garments are produced in a way that respects both people and the planet.

10

Chapter 10: The Future of Adaptive Fashion

Adaptive fashion is an emerging concept that aims to create clothing that is both stylish and functional, catering to the diverse needs of consumers. In the digital era, adaptive fashion is becoming increasingly important as designers seek to create garments that can adjust to changing weather conditions, body shapes, and lifestyles. This chapter explores the future of adaptive fashion and highlights some inspiring stories of brands that are leading the way in this area.

One exciting development in adaptive fashion is the use of smart textiles that can adjust to changing weather conditions. Companies like Google and Levi's have collaborated to create clothing that integrates technology with everyday wear. Their Project Jacquard resulted in a denim jacket that can control your smartphone, offering a glimpse into the future of fashion where technology and clothing are seamlessly integrated. This not only adds convenience but also reduces the need for multiple garments, promoting a more sustainable approach to fashion consumption.

Another innovative approach to adaptive fashion is the use of modular clothing, which allows consumers to customize and reconfigure their garments to suit different occasions and needs. Brands like Morph have been pioneers in this field, creating modular clothing that can be easily transformed and adapted. Their innovative designs not only offer versatility and functionality but also promote a more sustainable approach to fashion by reducing the need for multiple garments.

The digital era has also facilitated the development of virtual fitting rooms, which enable consumers to try on clothes without leaving their homes. This technology not only enhances the shopping experience but also reduces the need for physical samples and returns, minimizing the environmental impact of fashion production and consumption. Brands like Gucci and Tommy Hilfiger have embraced virtual fitting rooms, offering customers a new level of convenience and personalization.

11

Chapter 11: Sustainable Fashion Entrepreneurship: Building a Better Future

The rise of sustainable fashion has created new opportunities for entrepreneurs who are passionate about making a positive impact on the industry and the environment. This chapter explores the stories of visionary entrepreneurs who have built successful businesses centered around sustainability and highlights the challenges and rewards of pursuing a sustainable fashion venture.

One inspiring story is that of Eileen Fisher, who founded her eponymous brand in 1984 with a commitment to creating timeless, high-quality garments that are both stylish and sustainable. Eileen Fisher's dedication to environmental and social responsibility has been evident in every aspect of her business, from the materials used in her collections to the production processes employed in her factories. Her brand has set a high standard for the industry and demonstrated that it is possible to build a successful business while prioritizing sustainability.

The digital era has also facilitated the growth of sustainable fashion entrepreneurship by providing platforms for emerging designers and brands to reach a global audience. Online marketplaces like Etsy and Shopify have made it easier for entrepreneurs to launch and scale their businesses, connecting them with consumers who are seeking unique, eco-friendly products. These platforms have also fostered a sense of community among sustainable fashion entrepreneurs, encouraging collaboration and innovation.

Another important aspect of sustainable fashion entrepreneurship is the emphasis on ethical supply chains. Entrepreneurs like Safia Minney, founder of People Tree, have built their businesses on the principles of fair trade and transparency. By working closely with artisans and farmers in developing countries, Minney has created a brand that not only produces beautiful, sustainable garments but also empowers the people who make them. Her commitment to ethical production has set a high standard for the industry and inspired others to adopt similar practices.

As the demand for sustainable fashion continues to grow, it is essential for entrepreneurs to embrace this opportunity and build businesses that prioritize environmental and social responsibility. By focusing on sustainability, quality, and ethical production, entrepreneurs can create successful ventures that have a positive impact on the industry and the planet. The journey towards climate chic is not just about creating stylish garments but also about building a better future for all.

12

Chapter 12: The Role of Education in Promoting Sustainable Fashion

Education plays a crucial role in promoting sustainable fashion by raising awareness about the environmental and social impact of the industry and encouraging individuals to make more conscious choices. This chapter explores the importance of education in driving positive change and highlights some inspiring stories of initiatives that are working to educate and empower consumers, designers, and industry professionals.

One notable example is the Fashion Revolution movement, which was founded in response to the Rana Plaza factory collapse in 2013. Fashion Revolution advocates for greater transparency and accountability in the fashion industry, encouraging consumers to ask brands, "Who made my clothes?" Through their educational campaigns and resources, Fashion Revolution has raised awareness about the need for ethical and sustainable practices and inspired individuals around the world to take action.

The digital era has also facilitated the growth of educational initiatives that promote sustainable fashion. Online courses, webinars, and social media platforms have made it easier for individuals to access information and resources about sustainability. Programs like the Sustainable Fashion Academy and the Copenhagen Fashion Summit offer valuable educational opportunities for industry professionals, providing them with the knowledge and skills needed to drive positive change within their organizations.

In addition to formal education, grassroots initiatives and community projects play a vital role in promoting sustainable fashion. Local workshops and events provide opportunities for individuals to learn about sustainable practices and connect with like-minded people. Initiatives like the Fashion for Good Experience in Amsterdam offer interactive exhibits and activities that educate visitors about the impact of fashion on the environment and inspire them to make more conscious choices.

As education continues to play a crucial role in promoting sustainable fashion, it is essential for individuals and organizations to embrace these opportunities and work towards creating a more environmentally and socially responsible industry. By raising awareness and providing valuable resources, education can empower individuals to make more conscious choices and drive positive change within the fashion industry. The journey towards climate chic is not just about creating stylish garments but also about fostering a deeper understanding of the impact of our choices and the importance of sustainability.

13

Chapter 13: Collaborative Efforts for a Sustainable Future

The challenges posed by climate change and environmental degradation require collaborative efforts from all stakeholders in the fashion industry. This chapter explores the importance of collaboration in promoting sustainable fashion and highlights some inspiring stories of partnerships that have driven positive change.

One notable example is the Global Fashion Agenda, a non-profit organization that brings together industry leaders, policymakers, and NGOs to drive sustainability in fashion. Through initiatives like the Copenhagen Fashion Summit and the CEO Agenda, the Global Fashion Agenda fosters collaboration and innovation, encouraging stakeholders to work together towards a more sustainable future. Their efforts have not only raised awareness about the need for sustainability but also led to tangible commitments and actions from some of the world's leading fashion brands.

The digital era has also facilitated greater collaboration within the fashion industry, enabling brands, designers, and consumers to connect and share ideas. Online platforms and social media have provided spaces for dialogue and exchange, fostering a sense of community and collective responsibility. Initiatives like the Sustainable Apparel Coalition and the Fashion Pact have leveraged these digital tools to promote collaboration and drive positive change.

Another important aspect of collaboration is the involvement of consumers in the sustainability journey. Brands like Patagonia have built strong relationships with their customers, encouraging them to become advocates for environmental stewardship. Through initiatives like the Worn Wear program and the Patagonia Action Works platform, Patagonia has empowered consumers to take an active role in promoting sustainability and driving positive change.

As the fashion industry continues to face the challenges of climate change, it is essential for all stakeholders to work together towards a more sustainable future. By fostering collaboration and innovation, we can create a fashion industry that prioritizes environmental and social responsibility. The journey towards climate chic is not just about individual efforts but also about collective action and shared goals.

14

Chapter 14: The Role of Policy and Regulation in Sustainable Fashion

Policy and regulation play a crucial role in promoting sustainable fashion by setting standards and creating incentives for environmentally and socially responsible practices. This chapter explores the importance of policy and regulation in driving positive change and highlights some inspiring stories of initiatives that have made a significant impact.

One notable example is the Fashion Act in New York, which aims to hold fashion companies accountable for their environmental and social impact. The act requires brands to disclose information about their supply chains, carbon emissions, and labor practices, promoting greater transparency and accountability. By setting clear standards and expectations, the Fashion Act has encouraged brands to adopt more sustainable practices and demonstrated the potential for policy to drive positive change.

The digital era has also facilitated the development of policy and regulation that promotes sustainability in fashion. Online platforms and social media have provided spaces for advocacy and engagement, enabling individuals and organizations to raise awareness about the need for policy action. Initiatives like the Make Fashion Circular campaign by the Ellen MacArthur Foundation have leveraged these digital tools to promote circular fashion and advocate for policy changes that support sustainability.

Another important aspect of policy and regulation is the promotion of fair labor practices. Laws and regulations that protect workers' rights and ensure fair wages and safe working conditions are essential for creating an ethical fashion industry. Brands like Fair Trade USA have been at the forefront of promoting fair labor practices, certifying products that meet rigorous social and environmental standards. Their efforts have not only improved the lives of workers but also demonstrated the importance of policy and regulation in driving positive change.

As the fashion industry continues to face the challenges of climate change and social inequality, it is essential for policymakers and industry leaders to work together towards a more sustainable future. By setting clear standards and creating incentives for environmentally and socially responsible practices, policy and regulation can drive positive change and promote a more ethical and sustainable fashion industry. The journey towards climate chic is not just about individual efforts but also about systemic change and collective action.

15

Chapter 15: The Journey Ahead: Embracing Climate Chic

The journey towards climate chic is an ongoing process that requires continuous innovation, collaboration, and commitment from all stakeholders in the fashion industry. This final chapter explores the future of sustainable fashion and highlights the importance of embracing climate chic as a way of life.

One inspiring story is that of the brand Pangaia, which has built its business on the principles of sustainability and innovation. Pangaia's commitment to using eco-friendly materials and sustainable production methods is evident in every aspect of their brand. From their biodegradable packaging to their use of plant-based dyes, Pangaia has set a high standard for the industry and demonstrated the potential for sustainable fashion to become mainstream.

The digital era has also facilitated the growth of sustainable fashion by providing platforms for emerging designers and brands to reach a global audience. Online marketplaces like Moda Operandi and Farfetch have made it easier for consumers to discover and support sustainable fashion brands, promoting a more eco-friendly approach to fashion consumption. These platforms have also fostered a sense of community among sustainable fashion enthusiasts, encouraging collaboration and innovation.

As we look to the future, it is essential for the fashion industry to continue prioritizing sustainability and embracing climate chic. By making conscious choices and supporting brands that prioritize environmental and social responsibility, we can drive positive change and promote a more sustainable future. The journey towards climate chic is not just about creating stylish garments but also about fostering a deeper understanding of the impact of our choices and the importance of sustainability.

The future of fashion lies in our ability to adapt and evolve, ensuring that style and sustainability go hand in hand. By embracing climate chic, we can create a fashion industry that not only looks good but also does good for the planet. The journey ahead is challenging, but with innovation, collaboration, and commitment, we can build a better future for all.

Book Description: Climate Chic: Adaptive Fashion in a Digital Era explores the transformative journey of the fashion industry in response to climate change, emphasizing sustainability and innovative design. The book delves into the rise of eco-friendly materials, fashion tech innovations, and the importance of ethical production. It highlights the shift towards circular fashion, the impact of consumer behavior, and the emergence of digital fashion shows as sustainable alternatives.

Through engaging stories and real-world examples, readers will discover how brands and entrepreneurs are leading the way in promoting sustainability. The book also emphasizes the role of education, collaboration, and policy in driving positive change within the industry.

Ultimately, **Climate Chic** is a call to action for designers, consumers, and industry leaders to embrace adaptive fashion and prioritize environmental and social responsibility. It paints a hopeful picture of a future where style and sustainability coexist, paving the way for a more ethical and eco-friendly fashion industry.

www.ingramcontent.com/pod-product-compliance
Lightning Source LLC
LaVergne TN
LVHW020501080526
838202LV00057B/6093